auto racing's new wave

Jeff Gordon

Rainbow Warrior

By
Mark Stewart

The Millbrook Press
Brookfield, Connecticut

M

THE MILLBROOK PRESS

Produced by
BITTERSWEET PUBLISHING
John Sammis, President
and
TEAM STEWART, INC.

Series Design and Electronic Page Makeup by
JAFFE ENTERPRISES
Ron Jaffe

Researched and Edited by Mariah Morgan

All photos courtesy AP/ Wide World Photos, Inc. except the following:
SportPics: David Durochik, photographer — Cover
John Mahoney — Pages 10, 16, 17, 18, 21–top left,
21–bottom right, 22, 23, 26, 33
The following images are from the collection of Team Stewart:
NASCAR (© 1972) — Page 6
The Upper Deck Co. (© 1996) — Page 11
World of Outlaws (© 1987) — Page 20
JR Maxx (© 1991) — Page 30
Beckett Publications, Inc. (© 1995) — Page 35
Time, Inc. (© 1997) — Page 41
Racer Communications (© 1998) — Page 42

Printed in the United States of America

Published by
The Millbrook Press, Inc.
2 Old New Milford Road
Brookfield, Connecticut   06804

www.millbrookpress.com

Cataloging in Publication (CIP)
data for this title is on file
at the Library of Congress.

0-7613-1871-2 (lib. bdg.)
0-7613-1385-0 (pbk.)

pbk: 1 3 5 7 9 10 8 6 4 2
lib: 1 3 5 7 9 10 8 6 4 2

Contents

The Need for Speed

"He didn't know the meaning of the word No."
— JEFF'S MOM, CAROL

eff Gordon has been winning races since the day he was born. As a matter of fact, the first person he ever beat to the "finish line" was the doctor whose job it was to deliver him. Carol Gordon was in the midst of a slow and uncomfortable labor when her obstetrician decided to leave the hospital and tend to more urgent matters. He planned to return as soon as she showed signs of being ready to give birth. A few hours later, without much warning, Jeff "hit the accelerator." With the help of a midwife, Jeff came into this world on an August day in 1971, while his doctor was still miles away.

A month or so after Jeff was born, Carol and her husband, Will, were divorced. Their marriage had become unhappy, and Carol decided it would be better to raise Jeff and his older sister, Kim, by herself. Kim was a dream—she minded her mother, stayed

Though Jeff is still in his 20s, he has been competing in auto racing for more than 20 years.

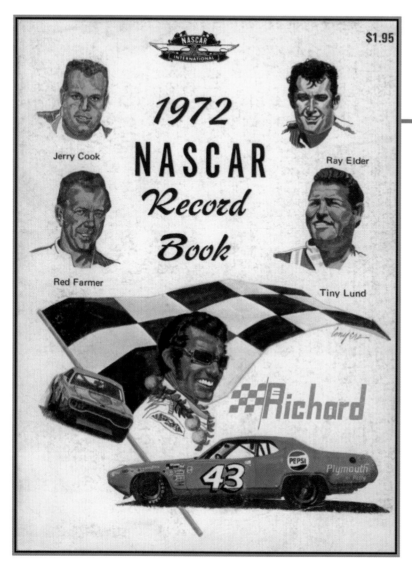

Jerry Cook

Ray Elder

1972 NASCAR Record Book

Red Farmer

Tiny Lund

$1.95

Richard

PEPSI 43 Plymouth

Richard Petty graces the cover of the 1972 NASCAR record book. Jeff's first Winston Cup race, in 1991, would be Petty's last.

out of danger, and almost never made a mess. Jeff, on the other hand, was quite a handful. When Carol tried to discourage Jeff from doing something, he just became more determined to do it. Also, he was constantly in motion. His mother would turn her back on the boy, and in an instant he would be gone. Jeff simply could not sit still. He did not like to be read to, and he was not very interested in TV. He always wanted to be involved in some kind of activity.

Jeff's need for speed began before he reached his third birthday. He skipped tricycles and training wheels and went straight to a two-wheeler. Soon he was riding his bike at breakneck speeds down the hill behind his house in Vallejo, California. He also rode in a pack with the older boys in the neighborhood. They rode their BMX bikes on a course a few streets away. Jeff was not only the youngest rider, but also small for his age. The other kids kind of "adopted" him and, at first, discouraged him from copying some of the more dangerous stunts they performed. But in no time Jeff was doing things on his bike that they were too scared to do on theirs.

Jeff's bike, by the way, was the most envied in the neighborhood. Because he was so small, he had to take the tiniest two-wheeler and modify it to make it even tinier. It was very little, but very cool. The modifications were made by John Bickford, his stepfather. John had become friendly with Carol when they met at the medical supply company where she was employed. He admired how hard she worked, raising two young children on her own. At first, John just stopped by to help out with the kids. Then, the two started dating. Their first date took place at a racetrack, and both Jeff and Kim went along.

After John and Carol were married, Jeff got into organized bicycle racing. John acted as Jeff's "crew chief." He owned a small company that manufactured products for the disabled, so he had a firm grasp of engineering. John made changes to Jeff's bike and suggested strategies for defeating the older kids. His stepfather encouraged him, and tried to teach him that the best way to achieve things in life is to set goals and go after them with every bit of energy and determination you've got. Jeff took this philosophy to heart, and by the age of four he was winning races against seven-, eight-, and nine-year-olds!

When the kids lined up to start a race, it was very easy to spot Jeff. He was half the size of his competition, and he could not reach the ground

Did You Know?

If Jeff had washed out as a racer, he might have become a musician. His uncle was the lead trumpet player in Elvis Presley's band.

with both feet. As soon as the starter gave the *Go* signal, Jeff would shoot into the lead, pedaling furiously on his tiny bike and doing everything he could to stay ahead of the older boys. If they caught him, he was in trouble—they would cut him off and drive him from the course.

Jeff's mother was terrified every time he entered a race. Often, Jeff would end up at the bottom of a pile, and she would hold her breath until she was sure he was okay. And every Saturday, it seemed as if some poor kid ended up in the hospital with a broken wrist or cracked rib. John Bickford knew how worried Carol was, and he agreed that BMX racing was a dangerous sport for a five-year-old. So he brought home something new for Jeff to drive: a car.

Full Throttle

"I started when I was five years old in quarter-midget racing."

— JEFF GORDON

eff's first race car was a quarter-midget. Quarter-midgets are low to the ground, with small tires and a number of safety features, including a sturdy rollbar. Their engines produce enough horsepower to propel them around a track at speeds around 25 miles per hour (40 kilometers per hour)—not very fast but certainly fast enough for even the most adventurous five-year-old. Fewer kids get hurt racing quarter-midgets than bikes, so Jeff's mother was happy about the switch.

John Bickford took his stepson to the Solano County Fairgrounds, where they hacked out an official-length (one-fifth of a mile) quarter-midget oval from an unused, overgrown parking lot. He told Jeff that he would not let him race until he knew every inch of the car, and could hear it "speak" to him. At first, the car was too much for Jeff to handle. He slipped all over the course, and had trouble steering through the curves without slowing down.

The limited speed and extra safety features of quarter-midget racers convinced Jeff's mother that he would be better off driving a car than riding a BMX bike.

Every evening, John and Jeff went to the course, and Jeff would drive his car until the engine was too hot to continue. Over the next few months, he and his little car became one. He could run a few laps and tell his stepfather what did not feel right, and exactly what adjustments it needed. After Jeff had run thousands of laps, John decided he was ready to begin racing.

Every weekend, somewhere in California, there was a quarter-midget meet. And almost every weekend, John and Jeff would drive there to compete. Often, they slept in the back of the family pickup. Jeff was by far the youngest racer on the circuit, and it showed. "I didn't do that well in my first year of competition," he remembers.

Jeff tended to push his car too hard in the curves, and he spun out a lot. Still, he was having a great time. And slowly but surely, he began to recognize how far he could push himself and his car without pushing too hard. "Once I got it straight in my head how to do this stuff," he says, "I started winning."

Indeed, as Jeff learned about controlling the forces involved in racing, his age and size became less of an obstacle and more of an advantage. Because Jeff carried far less weight in his car than his competitors—and because all the cars in his class were essentially the same size—he could move faster than anyone on the track. In the qualifying stages of a meet, when drivers race against the clock, Jeff almost always turned in the fastest time.

Because of his great qualifying times, Jeff was made to start most races in the back of the pack. This forced him to learn how to weave his way through the field during a race—one of the biggest challenges a young driver faces. Often, Jeff would get within a few feet of the lead cars when the race would end. He collected a lot of fast-time ribbons, but usually went home empty-handed because most races only gave out first-place trophies.

Jeff's mother saw how disappointed he was, and knew that no matter how many hours he practiced, he would never be able to learn the tricks needed to pass cars quickly. So she asked her husband to buy *her* a car. Over the next few months, she and Jeff raced around the track at the fairgrounds. Carol would try to block her son, while Jeff "read" her car and developed a set of slick moves to pass her.

Jeff, not yet six years old, could now run a race full-throttle—he almost never had to slow down.

This trading card features an early shot of Jeff behind the wheel of a quarter-midget. Once he learned how to control this type of car, his lack of size and weight became a great advantage.

QUALIFYING

Picking up Speed

UPPER DECK ™

Moving Up

chapter

"All the other parents were saying Jeff was probably lying about his age, that he was probably 20, and just really little."

— JOHN BICKFORD

y 1977, Jeff was killing the clock in qualifying, then destroying the competition in the regular races. In 1978, he recorded the fastest time in every qualifier he entered, won an amazing 35 main events, and set speed records on five different tracks. Jeff raced every weekend that year, which was unusual for a six-year-old. In 1979, Jeff joined the national quarter-midget circuit. Despite being several years younger than the other competitors—and much, much smaller—he was the most intimidating driver in his sport. Incredibly, he won 52 events that season, including the Grand National Championship in Denver, Colorado. Jeff was so good that other top drivers began pulling out of races he entered.

Did You Know?

Jeff lost count years ago, but he estimates that he has won more than 600 races in his career.

In an attempt to keep these kids interested, promoters began offering second- and third-place trophies for the first time.

By 1980, Jeff was as close to a professional racer as a child could be. His school ran on a "nine weeks on, three weeks off" schedule, so he raced locally during the nine school weeks and then entered national events during his three-week vacations. At the end of his "vacations," Jeff would fly home by himself so he would not miss class, while John drove the cars back in the trailer. Jeff was now competing in the highest-level events, beating teenagers and regularly setting course records.

Obviously, it was time to move to a more challenging vehicle. In 1981, Jeff began racing go-karts. These cars are much larger than quarter-midgets, have more than triple the power, and run on larger and trickier dirt tracks. The top drivers Jeff faced on the go-kart circuit were 15 and older, and they were not at all happy to see an undersized nine-year-old try to break into their ranks. At every opportunity, it seemed, they would try to intimidate Jeff, both on and off the track. "I really had to work hard, because the other drivers were tough," he says. "And they didn't want some newcomer coming in and winning."

Jeff answered the only way he knew how: He entered 25 events and won them all.

Go-karts may look small, but their engines pack plenty of horsepower.

Sprinting to Stardom

"Nobody was fool enough to drive that young, so they didn't think they needed an age rule."

— JEFF GORDON

eff Gordon was so good, it was boring to watch him. Any race he entered, regardless of the competition, he won. Even Jeff was getting bored. Quarter-midgets felt like amusement park rides. Go-karts were more fun, but presented little challenge. Jeff's parents were concerned that, just when he was ready to do something special in his sport, he would turn away from it.

For a while, this was true. Jeff became interested in water skiing, and as a result spent less time racing. This new sport gave him the speed and adrenaline rush he craved, while also challenging his creativity. After just a few weeks in ski school, Jeff's coaches told his parents that he was good enough to go pro! But his first love was still racing—he could not imagine himself doing anything but that. The question was, where do you go from go-karts?

Jeff takes a Sea Doo for a spin at Sea World in Orlando, Florida. Jeff has loved high-speed watersports since he went to water-skiing school as a teenager.

The answer had been there all along: sprint cars. Jeff was a huge fan of this sport, and after his own races he and his stepfather would often go watch the sprint races. His all-time hero, in fact, was a man named Steve Kinser, whom many believed was the best driver in sprint-car history. However, the idea of Jeff, now 13, getting behind the wheel of one of these machines seemed crazy at first. Sprint cars are full-size automobiles with 700-horsepower engines—70 times more powerful than go-karts—and reach speeds of 100 miles per hour (160 kilometers per hour) and more. Sprint-car racing is an all-out, full-throttle event. It is dangerous for even the most experienced driver.

Jeff's stepfather talked a buddy into building a sprint car that would accommodate Jeff's small proportions. When it arrived, they took it to a deserted road so Jeff could try it out. They had to—Jeff was still three years short of 16, which is the minimum

> *"You get to be 12 years old and you realize you've been in quarter midgets for eight years. What's next? I was getting older, not knowing what I wanted to do next."*
>
> **JEFF GORDON**

age for a California driver's license. Though intimidated by the raw power and size of his car when he first climbed behind the wheel, Jeff felt like he belonged there.

Unable to race legally in California, Jeff had to look for a circuit that did not have a minimum-age requirement. The best one was the All-Star sprint-car series in Florida. In February 1985, John and Jeff drove across the country to Jacksonville. "People were looking at us like we were crazy when they found out I was the driver," Jeff recalls.

When race officials saw how small Jeff was, they tried to keep him off the track. They claimed he would be overwhelmed, and that he might hurt himself and others. Jeff and his stepfather insisted that he was ready, and that there were no rules specifically forbidding 13-year-olds to race. In the end, they let Jeff race.

When the starting light flashed green, Jeff found himself in an unfamiliar situation. Everyone was roaring

Did You Know?

Jeff's first sprint-car win came in 1986 in Chillicothe, Ohio. The KC Speedway was one of the few outside Florida that would allow him to compete at 14.

past him, and he felt confused and scared. He slammed his foot on the accelerator and

Jeff skids through a turn in his sprint car during a 1988 race.

promptly lost control of his car. Jeff managed to swerve left just before hit the wall, causing only minor damage. A sudden cloudburst ended the race right after it began, so Jeff's poor start was wiped from the record books. But he never forgot that first terrifying experience. "These guys were flying past me like rockets," he remembers. "I was scared to death."

By the next race, across the state in Tampa, Jeff had time to relax and realize that he had simply had a case of the jitters. Deep down, he knew he could take the race to the older guys on the circuit. Over the next few weeks, he proved it, finishing as high as second. During this time, Jeff attracted national media attention for the first time, as ESPN ran a short profile of him.

Sprint-car legend Steve Kinser

In 1986, Jeff returned to Tampa—this time as one of the circuit's most popular "veterans." The 14-year-old only finished fourth, but it was one of his most memorable days in racing. Leading the pack early, Jeff valiantly held off a number of challenges, including one by his hero, Steve Kinser. In the end, the pack caught and passed him. After the race, Jeff saw Kinser approaching him, and immediately feared that he had done something wrong. As it turned out, Kinser was there to pay him a compliment. He told Jeff he was going to be a great driver. "Even today," claims Jeff, "I rate that as one of the highlights of my racing career."

Major Changes

chapter

*"This is it. This is
what I want to do."*

— JEFF GORDON

ecause Jeff was still underage, his sprint-car racing was confined to a few tracks in the Midwest and Florida. Going back and forth from their home in California was tiring and expensive for John and Jeff, so they purchased a small house in Pittsboro, Indiana, near the city of Indianapolis. Carol and Kim joined them there at the end of 1986.

The family struggled over the next few years. The prize money Jeff earned was barely enough to keep his car running. Carol worked to pay the household bills. And John did whatever he could—including working on other race cars—to help make ends meet. There were no motel rooms or fancy meals when Jeff went to a race, and often they made their own parts instead of buying them. It was a tough life with a lot of sacrifices. Does Jeff ever wish he had more of childhood? "There's definitely some things we missed out on," he concedes. "But I don't think it's anything I could look back on now and wish I'd done."

Did You Know?

In 1987, Jeff entered a series of sprint races called the World of Outlaws. These events were promoted by the drivers themselves, and some of the top people in the sport competed. That year, World of Outlaws issued its own trading card set, which featured Jeff's "rookie" card.

Jeff's next challenge was to be a normal teenager and a world-class driver at the same time. He attended Tri-West High School during the week and raced on the weekends. With a more restrictive school schedule than he had in California, Jeff was forced to stay closer to home. He adopted the nearby Bloomington Speedway as his "home track," and became one of the most feared drivers there. In 1988, he traveled to Australia and New Zealand to check out the sprint-car competition Down Under, and returned with 14 victories in the 15 events he entered.

In 1989, as Jeff neared his high-school graduation, he joined the USAC (United States Automobile Club) sprint circuit, which is considered the sport's "major league." In no time, Jeff won his first major U.S. sprint-car race in Florence, Kentucky. He also raced midget cars for the first time. Often, Jeff would compete in both midget and

Jeff waves to the crowd after his first USAC sprint-car victory.

sprint events in the same weekend. Though a notch below sprint cars, midgets are fast and fun to drive. Jeff won his first race in a midget, and went on to earn USAC Midget Rookie of the Year honors. In 1990, he won the USAC National Midget Championship, becoming the youngest driver ever to do so at the age of 19. In 1991, he began experimenting with Dirt Cars, which look a lot like the old-time cars that raced at the Indianapolis 500. He finished the year as champion in this division, once again being the youngest ever to do so.

All the years of hard work and penny-pinching were about to pay off. Jeff announced that he was ready to commit to one kind of car, and no one doubted that he would be extremely good at whatever type of racing he chose. Sponsors were lining up to pay him big bucks, so all he had to do was make up his mind.

This was not as easy as he thought. When Jeff was a kid, he raced for fun. Now he was about to make a decision that might affect the rest of his life. One of his options was stock-car racing, which

Jeff poses with the trophy he won in his first-ever midget-car race.

Jeff, 18, shows off his USAC Rookie of the Year award.

features ultra-powerful versions of "stock" cars that you might see in the window of the local automobile dealership.

Jeff and his mother flew to North Carolina, to visit the legendary Buck Baker's driving academy. Jeff got behind the wheel, took off, and was in love. Stock cars weigh almost four times more than sprint cars, but despite their size they are smooth and powerful. Jeff called his stepfather and told him to sell all of their cars and equipment. From that moment on, he was a stock-car driver. "The car was different from anything that I was used to," he remembers. "It was so big and heavy. It felt very fast, but very smooth. I loved it."

Jeff poses with his "team" (from left, car owner Rollie Hemling, car builder John East, and stepfather John Bickford) after winning midget and sprint titles in the same day at a 1990 event.

The Race Begins

chapter 6

> *"I caught this white car out of the corner of my eye...I said, 'Man, that guy's going to wreck!'"*
> — RICK HENDRICK

The difference between wanting to race stock cars and actually *doing* it can be a problem, even for someone as talented as Jeff Gordon. It costs millions of dollars to hire a pit crew and keep a car on the road for a season, and there are only so many sponsors willing to do this. Also, there are a limited number of starting spots available in each event, so there are no guarantees that a car will even be *in* a given race. For these reasons, investors prefer an older driver behind the wheel of their car.

Luckily for Jeff, a man named Hugh Connerty happened to be at Baker's Academy during Jeff's visit. He owned the car sponsored by the Outback Steakhouse chain, and

Did You Know?

In Jeff's first Busch Series race, he crashed into the car driven by the son of his driving-school instructor.

already had an excellent young crew chief named Ray Evernham. Now he needed a dri-

NASCAR's dynamic duo: driver Jeff Gordon and crew chief Ray Evernham.

ver. When he saw how Jeff handled his car—and found out it was first-time driving—he immediately signed Jeff for the remainder of the 1990 season.

When Jeff met Ray Evernham, they hit it off immediately. Jeff asked the right questions and listened attentively to the answers. Ray's focus and determination reminded Jeff of his stepfather's. The pair teamed up to run the final four races of the Busch Series, which is the second-highest tier of competition sanctioned by the National Association for Stock Car Automobile Racing (NASCAR).

Jeff performed well enough in 1990 to attract the attention of Bill Davis, whose car was sponsored by Carolina Ford Dealers. Davis was interested in hiring Jeff for the

Jeff accepts USAC's 1991 Silver Crown award.

1991 season. Jeff told him he wanted to be Busch Rookie of the Year in 1991, and win the series championship in 1992. Davis liked his confidence and they formed a team. Jeff performed as promised, placing in the Top 10 nine times and edging out David Green as the circuit's top newcomer. The following year, Jeff drove for Davis again, in a car sponsored by Baby Ruth. He had a shot at the title, but fell just short, finishing fourth overall. Still, it was an impressive beginning for a 22-year-old competing against drivers with 10 to 20 years of experience.

During Jeff's marvelous 1992 season, he caught the eye of millionaire car owner Rick Hendrick. Like Jeff, the 42-year-old Hendrick had accomplished much in a short time. Already, he was the nation's most successful auto dealer. Hendrick believed in the team approach to winning. His company employed 200 people to design, build, test, and race stock cars. As a businessman, he loved to discover bright young talent; as a former record-setting speedboat driver, he knew when someone was about to lose control and crash.

At the Atlanta 300, in March 1992, Hendrick saw Jeff snaking through the field and careening around the curves. He told everyone to stop and watch—there was no way this guy could keep driving like that without wrecking. Jeff continued to "drive loose" for the entire race, but never lost control. Jeff edged legends Dale Earnhardt and Harry Gant to win the race. Hendrick was impressed. "Who is that?" he asked. "That's that kid Gordon," someone answered.

Hendrick was even more impressed after meeting Jeff; he seemed to have it all. Smart, young, handsome, and successful—what more could you ask for? Other car owners were pursuing Jeff at this time, including Junior Johnson and Cale Yarbrough. No one doubted Jeff was ready to make the leap to the Winston Cup circuit, NASCAR's elite level.

Jeff's loyalties were with Bill Davis, who asked Jeff to be patient while he put together the money for a Carolina Ford Winston Cup team. When Davis failed to come through quickly enough, however, Jeff decided there was no time to lose. He and Ray Evernham signed with Hendrick Motorsports. Jeff took a lot of criticism for abandoning the man who had given him his first major break, but as Jeff is quick to point out, he was not "given" anything. Everything he had in racing he had earned. Still, Jeff feels bad about leaving Davis. "I've always wished success for Bill because I saw how hurt he was when everything happened," says Jeff. "But sometimes you have to separate friendship and business."

"You couldn't ask for a better driver— he's always got a great attitude."

RICK HENDRICK

Welcome to the Big Time

chapter 7

"Just getting to Winston Cup racing was a tremendous achievement."

— JEFF GORDON

Jeff began his Winston Cup career in the fall of 1992, finishing 31st in the season's final race, the Hooters 500. He became the number-three driver on the Hendrick Motorsports team, behind Ricky Rudd and Ken Schrader. Rudd left soon after to form his own team, so Jeff never really got to know him. Rudd's replacement, Terry Labonte, was someone Jeff knew well. The 1984 Winston Cup champion, Labonte was one of the circuit's top drivers. Schrader was a well-known "workhorse," who often entered two or three races a week. They had a lot to teach Jeff, who knew he still had plenty to learn.

One of Jeff's proudest days came when his new car was unveiled at the North Carolina Motor Speedway. A crowd of fans and reporters oohed and aahed when the tarp was pulled off to reveal a bright red Chevrolet with a band of blue, green, and yellow. The car, number 24, was sponsored by DuPont, which manufactures automotive finishes. In many ways, this moment marked a major change in the image of NASCAR. Jeff and his "rainbow warriors" were sending a signal to the grizzled old outlaws and

Jeff compares notes with teammate Terry Labonte.

gunslingers who ruled the stock-car world. From now on, the sport would be a lot slicker and a lot smarter.

And a lot younger. At 21, Jeff was entering a world ruled by drivers in their 30s, 40s, and 50s. The top names in NASCAR in 1992 were Dale Earnhardt (41), Darrell Waltrip (45), Bill Elliott (37), Rusty Wallace (36), Mark Martin (33), Dale Jarrett (36), Ernie Irvan (33), Kyle Petty (32), and Morgan Shepherd (51). These guys had paid their dues. They were not likely to take kindly to this baby-faced intruder.

When the 1993 season began, Jeff had three goals. He wanted to win a race, finish as Rookie of the Year, and end up in the Top 10 overall. Rick Hendrick told the press he would be happy if Jeff learned from the older drivers and won a couple of poles. The pole position is awarded to the fastest qualifier for a race—it is both an honor and an advantage, as the pole winner gets to start the race first and get a good pit location.

The year's first event was the 125-mile qualifier for the Daytona 500.

NASCAR veterans Bill Elliott (left) and Darrell Waltrip.

maxx '91

owner

Rick Hendrick

In auto racing, even team owners get their own trading cards. Rick Hendrick's cars had two wins and 19 Top 5 finishes the year this card was issued.

Technically, it only helps to determine starting positions in the big race. But because the Daytona 500 is NASCAR's most prestigious competition, merely winning a qualifier is considered a significant achievement, even though it does not count as an official win. When Jeff tore across the finish line ahead of everyone else, the crowd could barely believe it. Not since the early 1960s had a rookie won this event—and at 21, Jeff was by far its youngest winner. "I wasn't ready to win it," he admits. "But we did. Hey, you never know."

Jeff was so new to NASCAR that he did not know where to find "Victory Lane," the traditional path race winners follow to the presentation stand. Eventually, an embarrassed Jeff figured it out. He got out of the car, went to the podium, and waved to the fans. Jeff collected his trophy and a kiss from the new Miss Winston, Brooke Sealey.

It was love at first sight.

Jeff's first full year on the Winston Cup circuit was one for the books. At the start of the Daytona 500, he blasted out of the second row to become the first rookie ever to lead the race's first lap. He challenged for the lead throughout the afternoon, but in the final stages his inexperience showed and he slipped back to fifth. Still, a fifth-place finish at Daytona is something to be proud of.

Jeff learned more lessons as the year wore on—about passing, conserving fuel, "drafting" behind other cars—and finished among the leaders in other big races. Jeff won his first pole at the fall race in Charlotte, which was held just a few miles from his family's new home in western North Carolina. Although he reached one of his goals by being named Rookie of the Year in 1993, he finished 14th in the driver standings and could not do better than second in any race. "We were awful close to a win a few times," Jeff remembers, adding that despite a good year it was still disappointing to fall short of his other two goals.

Brooke gives Jeff a victory smooch after the 1994 Brickyard 400.

At the year-end NASCAR banquet in New York, Jeff received his award as top rookie. He then spent the night dancing with Brooke, whose duties as Miss Winston were officially over. When the other drivers saw these two kissing and cuddling, everything made sense. All season long, Jeff had been like a phantom—one second he was standing right next to you, the next moment he was gone. And everyone had wondered why he did not have a girlfriend. Obviously, he and Brooke had been seeing each other secretly. There was a strict rule forbidding Miss Winston to date any drivers, so they could not get caught. A few weeks later, he and Brooke announced that they planned to marry.

Jeff won his first outing in 1994, an event called the Busch Clash. It was an "all-star" exhibition featuring the previous year's pole winners. Jeff played the field like an old pro, waiting patiently for just the right chance and then flying by Brett Bodine and Dale Earnhardt for a down-to-the-wire victory. At the Daytona 500, Jeff improved on

The Gordon File

JEFF'S FAVORITE...

Food . . . . Pizza
Color . . . All the colors of the rainbow.
Charity . . . . The Leukemia Society.
"Leukemia takes the lives of more children than any other disease."
Ways to Relax . . . . . . Playing video games. "Video games can take the pressures off of racing. It's like my mind takes a vacation for an hour... or six!"
Video Game . . Jeff Gordon XS Racing

Jeff does not have a speedometer in his car. "It just breaks my concentration," he explains. "I know when I'm running good or not, just by feel."

his 1993 finish, coming in fourth. The middle of the season, however, saw his fortunes take a nosedive. For several weeks running, Jeff was unable to put together a solid, start-to-finish performance.

Ray Evernham knew his young driver was feeling down. He also heard the whispers: *Maybe this Gordon kid isn't so good*, people were saying. That made the crew chief angry. Jeff had more going for him on his worst day than a lot of drivers had on their best. He just needed a little luck.

At the Coca-Cola 600 in Charlotte, Evernham saw a chance to make his *own* luck. Jeff was in a three-way duel with veterans Rusty Wallace and Dale Jarrett with just a few laps to go. Each driver needed one more pit stop. As Jeff pulled into the pits, Evernham eyeballed his tires and instantly ordered his crew to "two-tire" the car. Instead of changing all four tires, they just did the rear ones. Jeff blew out of the pits a few seconds ahead of Wallace and gave it everything he had. Evernham held his breath, praying that the front tires would hold out.

When Jeff crossed the finish line less than four seconds ahead of Wallace, the Rainbow Warriors went wild. They had given their driver the lead, and he had made it stand up. Car number 24's first official Winston Cup win had been a true team effort. A couple of laps from the finish, Jeff knew he was going to win. He became so emotional that he began to weep. "I was trying not to hit the wall from all the tears that were coming down my face," Jeff remembers. "Getting that first win, especially in my own backyard, is a feeling I'll never forget."

Jeff's next triumph came at the inaugural Brickyard 400. The race was held at the Indianapolis Motor Speedway, which for more than 80 years had played host to the Indianapolis 500. Back when Jeff lived in Pittsboro, he visited the track and dreamed of racing there. The 1994 Brickyard 400 marked the first time that stock cars had ever raced on the world-famous track.

Jeff led for most of the race, which came down to a bumper-to-bumper duel with Ernie Irvan. Irvan was one of the most intelligent drivers on the circuit, and Jeff knew he might not survive a high-speed, cat-and-mouse game with the wily veteran. In the pits, Evernham calculated that Jeff might have a little more tread left on his tires than Irvan. The crew chief instructed Jeff to race side-by-side, so that Irvan could not draft behind him and conserve rubber. The strategy worked. With four laps remaining, Irvan's tire blew and Jeff pulled away for the win. The $613,000 paycheck was the largest in NASCAR history. That evening, Jeff and Brooke celebrated his victory in style—they watched a tape of the race and split a pizza.

Jeff waves to the crowd at the Indianapolis Motor Speedway.

Wonder Boy

chapter

"Jeff Gordon could race Formula One cars, and I think he'd win races there. He's that talented."

— TERRY LABONTE

eff finished the 1994 season ranked eighth among Winston Cup drivers, and was third in overall prize money. Dale Earnhardt finished on top of the heap for the second-straight year. As the 1995 season began, everyone was talking about their "rivalry." When Earnhardt jokingly called Jeff "Wonder Boy," things really heated up. In truth, the only rivalry that existed was between Jeff's fans and Dale's fans.

Jeff's fans were younger. They loved his squeaky-clean image and dramatic sense of style. Earnhardt appealed to older NASCAR

"He's not afraid of anything... he's got the talent and the team."
NASCAR SUPERSTAR DALE EARNHARDT

followers, who appreciated how long and hard he had worked to reach the top of his sport. They also got a kick out of his take-no-prisoners driving style. Earnhardt was called "The Intimidator," and with good reason. When you saw number 3 coming up behind you, you had to be ready for anything, including a 180-mile per hour (290-kilometers per hour) "love tap."

The year played out like a Hollywood movie, with both drivers distancing themselves from the competition, then going head-to-head for the Winston Cup championship. Earnhardt won five races, and finished either second or third 11

Jeff's dream season in 1995 was front-page news.

more times. Jeff won seven events and finished second of third nine times.

After winning the Mountain Dew Southern 500 in early September, Jeff owned a seemingly unbeatable 300-point lead over Earnhardt. But the rest of the year belonged to The Intimidator, who shaved Jeff's advantage down to just 34 points. Jeff held on in the season's final race and was crowned Winston Cup champion. When Jeff accepted top driver honors at the NASCAR banquet that December, he led the crowd in a toast to Earnhardt. Then he toasted Ray Evernham. And then John and Carol Bickford.

You can't win 'em all. Jeff is edged at the 1996 First Union 400 by teammate Terry Labonte, who went on to capture the Winston Cup title.

Earlier that year, Jeff brought in a team of professionals to manage his finances and see to the day-to-day details of his life. For the first time in 20 years, his folks were free to be regular people again.

Before he knew it, Jeff had to start planning to defend his title in 1996. He went about this task the best way he knew how: by winning as many races as he could. But the Winston Cup standings do not always favor the driver who wins the most. Consistency is just as important, and finishing in the Top 10 on a regular basis is often enough to challenge for the championship.

Jeff learned this fact the hard way in 1996. He won 10 races—twice as many as anyone else in the sport—yet still missed out on the Winston Cup title by a maddening 37 points. The man who beat him, Hendrick Motorsports teammate Terry Labonte, won only twice. But he finished in the Top 10 in 27 of 31 starts. Jeff turned in 24 Top 10 finishes, which just was not enough.

Hearin' It

Fans new to stock-car racing are sometimes amazed at how much, and how loudly, Jeff gets booed. That is the price he pays for being so good so young.

"He's good-looking, a gazillionaire, he has his own jet, a beautiful wife, and he wins more races than anybody," Ray Evernham once said. "If I weren't his best buddy, **I'd** be booing him, too!"

Jeff knows the people who boo him are simply fans of other drivers, and over time he has come to accept this as kind of a compliment. Besides, as Dale Earnhardt once told him, "As long as they're making noise, kid, you're okay."

"They're booing you because either you're winning too much or you're doing something you're not supposed to," says Jeff. "I have a smile on my face, because I must be doing something right. You listen to how much noise is being made when you're introduced, and you want the loudest and longest noise. Some of them are booing, some of them are cheering, and some of them don't know which way to go."

Back to Back

chapter

> *"Jeff Gordon is, undoubtedly, one of the greatest race car drivers ever to sit down in a car."*
> — MARK MARTIN

T he Daytona 500 is the "brass ring" every stock-car driver grabs for. It is held in the town where stock-car racing first flourished in the 1930s, and the place where NASCAR itself was born. As the first major race of the season, it enables the winner to say, "Catch me if you can!" and set the tone for the entire year. Jeff wanted to win the 1997 Daytona 500 in the worst way. Although he would never say it, he believed he had been, by far, the sport's top driver in 1996. Well, here was a chance to prove it.

Early in the race, it was Dale Earnhardt who took the lead. Daytona was the one crown that had eluded him in his illustrious career, and every year it seemed as if something weird kept him from winning. This year, it was a rare error on Earnhardt's part. Running alongside Jeff, he came out of a turn too high, nicked the wall, then bounced back and bumped into Jeff. This slowed Earnhardt down just enough to cause Dale Jarrett and Ernie Irvan to smash into him from behind. Car number 3 went tumbling off the track. Luckily Earnhardt was unhurt.

The race's new leader, Bill Elliott, had little time to enjoy his advantage. In his rearview mirror, he saw Jeff and his teammates, Terry Labonte and Ricky Craven, crowded behind him. He knew he was in trouble. Taking advantage of the powerful aerodynamics created by vehicles moving at these speeds, Jeff was being "pulled" by Elliott's car, and "pushed" by Labonte and Craven. Jeff could hit the accelerator at any time and blow right past him, and Elliott knew it. Jeff waited until they were six laps from the finish, then worked it so that *all three* Hendrick cars were able to pass the helpless Elliott at the same time. Jeff won, and his teammates took second and third. It was owner Rick Hendrick's dream come true, the ultimate example of teamwork at the highest level of NASCAR competition.

In April, Jeff earned the respect of many old-timers with two thrilling wins. In the Food City 500, he and Rusty Wallace went into the final turn side-by-side. They rubbed against each other all the way to the finish line, where Jeff nosed out a heart-stopping victory. The very next week, in Martinsville, Jeff survived a spinout, got back on the track, caught Bobby Hamilton with less than

> "I was dead meat, and I knew it—
> it was just a matter of when and where."
>
> **BILL ELLIOTT**

Jeff's win at Daytona got the ball rolling on another championship year.

a lap to go, and edged him for the checkered flag. It was the kind of hard-nosed driving that NASCAR fans love.

Jeff added a win at Darlington to his résumé in August, further impressing old-time fans. An ancient track with more lumps, bumps, and cracks than most city streets, Darlington was long considered the most challenging course in stock-car racing. Jeff held off all challengers to win a $1 million bonus for his third "major" victory of the year. The last driver to do that was Bill Elliott, back in 1985.

Jeff held the lead in the Winston Cup championship battle through the fall, but not by much. On the season's final weekend, Dale Jarrett and Mark Martin each had a chance to pass him. With 10 wins already under his belt for the second-straight year, Jeff could certainly be proud of what he had accomplished. But he wanted to be known as a guy who did not fade down the stretch, as he had in 1995 and '96.

A couple of stupid mishaps in practice and qualifying sent Jeff to the back of the pack for the start of the race. Tire trouble plagued him throughout the day, and he was barely able to limp across the finish line in 17th place. Jarrett, who raced beautifully, finished third. It was not enough, however, to catch Jeff in the points standings. Jeff held on to win his second Winston Cup title by a mere 14 points. Martin finished 15 points behind Jarrett. It was the closest 1-2-3 finish in history.

Jeff's goal for 1998 was to win back-to-back championships. NASCAR was celebrating its 50th year, which would make another Winston Cup title extraspecial. Jeff's main competition would come from Mark Martin, but the early part of the season belonged to Dale Earnhardt, who finally won the Daytona 500. Some detected a tear in The Intimidator's eye as he pulled into Victory Lane for the first time in 20 tries. Back in 1993, Dale had teased Jeff mercilessly for crying after a win. Yes, a slightly embarrassed Earnhardt admitted to reporters after Daytona, "I pulled a Gordon."

For the rest of the year, however, Jeff looked like he was "pulling an Earnhardt." Beginning with a thrilling win at the Coca-Cola 600 in late May, Jeff put together one of the most memorable seasons in auto racing history. At one point, the Rainbow Warriors scored 17 Top 5 finishes in a row, including five consecutive first-place finishes—an unheard-of feat in modern-day racing.

Did You Know?

After his third Winston Cup championship, Jeff finally felt like a member of "the club." A baby by NASCAR standards, he often felt the older drivers did not take him seriously. As he finished the year, he sensed this was beginning to change.

"I was really resented after the first championship, resented a little less after the second, and by the third one I was seeing even less resentment," he claims.

It was truly a team effort. When Evernham told Jeff he needed to get a little extra out of his engine or his tires, Jeff did what he had to do. When Jeff reported a problem to Evernham, he never failed to come up with a creative solution. And when car number 24 needed a lightning-fast pit stop, the Rainbow Warriors always came through.

Jeff ran away with the Winston Cup title, scoring an amazing 13 victories. No one in NASCAR's modern era had taken the checkered flag more often in a single season, and no one under 30 had ever won three NASCAR championships. Jeff's triumphs included wins at the Brickyard 400, Watkins Glen, Darlington, Rockingham, and Atlanta. During the year, he also moved into second place on NASCAR's all-time prize money list. As the sport's 50th season came to a close, there was little doubt who would lead the sport into its second half-century.

Jeff's trading cards are the hottest in the hobby.

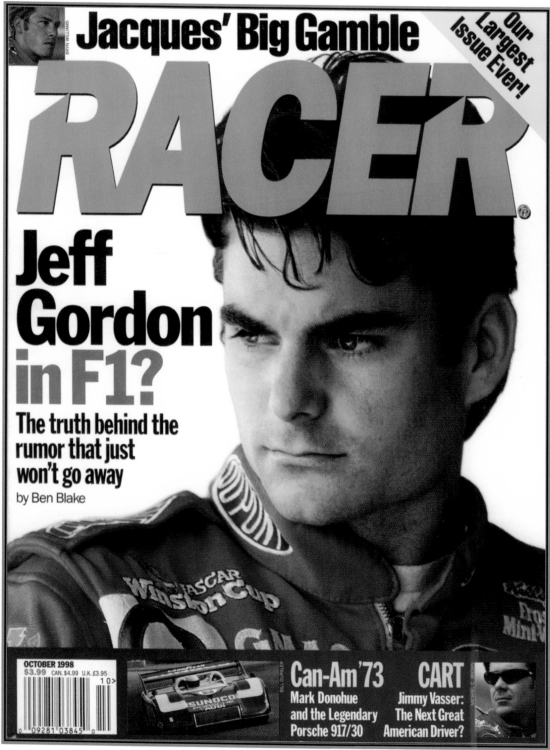

Jacques' Big Gamble

Our Largest Issue Ever!

RACER

Jeff Gordon in F1?

The truth behind the
rumor that just
won't go away

by Ben Blake

OCTOBER 1998
$3.99 CAN. $4.99 U.K. £3.95
10>
0 09281 03845 0

Can-Am '73
Mark Donohue
and the Legendary
Porsche 917/30

CART
Jimmy Vasser:
The Next Great
American Driver?

Some think Jeff's incredible record in open-wheel racing will one day lead him away from stock cars and into Formula One competition.

The Face of Racing

"I want to be involved in a sport as big as the NBA or the NFL, one that's recognized around the world."

— JEFF GORDON

When your life is like a little kid's dream, reality can sometimes be hard to take. That is why, despite being one of the most level-headed people on the planet, even Jeff was rattled by the events of 1999. First, he did not win his third-straight Winston Cup championship. That honor went to Dale Jarrett. Second, and far worse, was the shocking news in September that Ray Evernham was resigning as Jeff's crew chief.

Their partnership had produced three championships in four years, and their chemistry was unlike any other in the sport. Although both were young men by NASCAR standards, their partnership was the oldest on the circuit. As a crew chief, Evernham had accomplished everything. Now he wanted to be a car owner. Had Rick Hendrick offered him the position of general manager of all three of his teams, perhaps he would have stayed. But his days in the pits were over.

Jeff and crew chief Robbie Loomis discuss strategy for the 2000 Daytona 500.

Jeff tried to see the silver lining in this dark cloud. For years Jeff's critics claimed that Evernham was the real secret behind his success. Now he had a chance to prove them wrong. Yes, Jeff says, Ray was the leader of the Rainbow Warriors. However, the team they built together was strong enough to keep performing at a high level without him. Also, Jeff knows you cannot improve unless you are tested from time to time. "It's hard to get to where you need to until you go through some hard times," he says. "Then you can get a whole lot better feel for things."

Did You Know?

After Ray Evernham resigned from Jeff's crew, Robbie Loomis became the new chief of the Rainbow Warriors. "I'm sure a lot of people doubt us," says Jeff. "But we've got a team that really is enjoying working together."

The good news in 1999 was that Jeff won his second Daytona 500. It was a race that, years from now, may be considered the finest of Jeff's career. The entire field seemed to have one goal in mind: keep number 24 from winning. He was blocked, bumped, and bullied throughout the day, and it took brilliant driving just to stay on the track. With 12 laps remaining, Jeff was in third place, right on Dale Earnhardt's bumper. Suddenly he darted inside and used an aerodynamic "push" by Earnhardt's teammate, Mike Skinner, to pull ahead, into second place.

Then, with just 10 laps remaining, Jeff made a move that will be replayed over and over again. As he and leader Rusty Wallace entered a turn, Jeff swerved all the way down to the apron and then zigzagged quickly back in front of Wallace, while barely

Jeff leads the pack into the first turn.
He started off the 2000 season by winning the pole at the Daytona 500.

career highlights

ACHIEVEMENT	YEAR
Quarter-Midget National Champion	1979, 1981
USAC Midget Rookie of the Year	1989
USAC Midget Rookie Champion	1990
Busch Series Rookie of the Year	1991
Busch Series Top Money Winner	1992
Winston Cup Rookie of the Year	1993
Brickyard 400 Winner	1994, 1998
Winston Cup Champion	1995, 1997, 1998
Daytona 500 Winner	1997, 1999
5 Consecutive NASCAR Victories	1998

missing the slower-moving Ricky Rudd. From there he kept Earnhardt on his bumper right to the finish line for a breathtaking victory. How did it feel to be the target of everyone on the track? "I don't expect any different," Jeff says. "It's almost like an honor."

Actually, the biggest honor came after Jeff took the checkered flag. Earnhardt pulled up alongside "Boy Wonder," bumped fenders, and waved. The Intimidator had been beaten fair and square—with a couple of maneuvers even *he* had to appreciate—and just wanted to let Jeff know he knew it.

Jeff finished the 1999 season sixth in the Winston Cup standings, which was definitely an "off" year. His fans are quick to point out that, with a circuit-leading seven victories, Jeff's disappointing season would be a dream season for most of the other drivers.

But Jeff is not like most other drivers. In fact, he is unlike anyone else in his sport. His blend of talent, personality, and youthful good looks has transformed stock-car racing from a noisy backwoods barbecue to a prime-time, major-league sport. In 2000, NASCAR began an ambitious partnership with NBC and FOX. It will bring racing into the homes of millions of Americans. And Jeff's is the face that millions of Americans want to see.

Despite more than 600 career wins—from quarter-midgets to stock cars—Jeff has an unquenchable thirst for victory. Who knows how many wins he will have when he retires?

Index

PAGE NUMBERS IN ITALICS REFER TO ILLUSTRATIONS.